Love from the Vortex
& Other Poems

Advance Praise for
Love from the Vortex & Other Poems

"Sealey-Ruiz opens a world to us in which we are reminded of the importance of speaking truthfully - with both love and rage—about our past and the lovers and loved ones who bring us to the present—and home."
Jacqueline Woodson, Author of *Red at the Bone*

"These poems are lighthouses. They are roadmaps. They are canaries returning from the coal mine with news of joyous survival. Dr. Yolanda Sealey-Ruiz has seen what stalks the blood of an unexamined self—one scared to walk into the beautiful ache of love—and here she is dazzlingly unafraid to show us 'what liberation looks like' on the other side. 'There is no shade / no place to retreat' from this telling, this raised glass to the glorious risk-and-recovery of life. Determined and compassionate and open, this is the voice of a poet who knows the heart and a scholar who knows the stakes. And good lord are we lucky to have it. Sealey-Ruiz's work should be within arms reach of every classroom in America."
Dr. Adam Falkner, Author of *The Willies*

"From the moment I opened this book, I was captivated and enamored with the beautiful ways Yolanda Sealey-Ruiz uses language to tell stories of love, stories of hope, stories of despair and then stories of love again. Throughout each poem, she shares her truths—truths that we can all relate to if we have ever been brave enough to love."
Dr. Gholdy Muhammad, Author of *Cultivating Genius*

"*Love from the Vortex* is an evocative book of poems that ceaselessly opens our hearts page after page. Dr. Sealey-Ruiz holds our hands and walks us through her journey of finding, losing and holding onto love. One falls out and falls back in love by the end of it. This is a must have for those of us who enjoy expanding our hearts while we read. Now more than ever, we need texts like this that remind us of the art of loving in full presence."
Angel Acosta, Founder of New York City Healing Collective

"*Love from the Vortex & Other Poems* is an earnest reminder of how humbling, trying and rewarding love is. Despite age or experience, *Love from the Vortex & Other Poems* resonates with anyone who has ever found, nurtured and lost love and serves as a comfort that love, no matter how fleeting, is a joy in itself and that loving and caring for oneself is the only way to get through and to get by. Yolanda Sealey-Ruiz is a true wordsmith and inspiration."
Brittany Maldonado, Artist

"*Love from the Vortex* represents the documentation and memorializing of how love can hurt and liberate one to continue to heal through loving themselves; while finding hope and patience in loving another. This book is for any woman who may have experienced pain in love and loving and who is uncertain of how to heal."
Dr. Cluny Lavache, Educational Leader

"I saw beauty in how the trauma of her experiences are met with Love and acceptance, cultivating a story of fond familiarity. Enabling the reader to glimpse inside some of her foundational experiences without the anxiety of regret or desire for answers, but rather, as they are. It's only right that she makes the vortex visible. I've danced with the vortex. Still do."
Patrick Williamson, Diversity, Equity & Inclusion Educator

"I was quite in awe of these poems. The poems are beautifully written. They are compelling, emotive, and evocative. They captured my soul and left me feeling vulnerable."
***Love from the Vortex* Reader**

Dear Patrice,

May peace and love surround you... always!.
Be Blessed.

Love from the Vortex
& Other Poems

Yolanda Sealey-Ruiz

Love is the answer! Yolie
3.2020.

Kaleidoscope Vibrations LLC
New York, New York
2020

Requests for permission to make copies of any part of
this book should be emailed to:
publishing.kvibrations@gmail.com

Printed in the United States of America.

ISBN 978-1-949949-02-5

Front cover image and illustrations by 19.
Book design by Caroline Rinaldy.

First printing, 2020

www.kvibrations.com

For me & the six.

I write to free & heal myself.
—YOLANDA SEALEY-RUIZ

Nobody has ever measured, not even poets,
how much the heart can hold.
—ZELDA FITZGERALD

Contents

Joseph

Ian

Angel

Salvador

Zaren

Tyrone

Other Poems

Joseph

13 Years of Admiration

*I really believe that there is an invisible red thread tied
between him and me, and that it has stretched and tangled
for years —across oceans and lifetimes. I know that it won't
break because our souls are tied.*
—JENNIFER ELISABETH,
BORN READY: UNLEASH YOUR INNER DREAM GIRL

MORE THAN FRIENDS

Something has certainly happened
between this week & last
between yesterday & today
within this last

      hour

            minute

                 moment.

Several hours of my day
are spent
thinking of you—
What you

      look like

            smell like

                 smile like.

& I want to be near you
      or that instant
      or that moment;
tell you that a friendship
like ours can only remain
if we agree to never
look into each other's eyes...

THIS MOMENT

Something has shifted

                    between us.

                              I write very little now,

you even less.

                    Perhaps it's the quickened

                              pace of our lives

that has prevented

                    our connection.

                              Or was it the movie?

In all of its delicious darkness,

                    did it reveal an adventure

                              you're not prepared to take?

Maybe the flame ignited on that

                    frigid Wednesday evening

                              has slowly fizzled for you...

has it?

It hasn't for me. . .

Why won't you answer me?

In some ways, the fire burns

brighter than ever before.

A white hot pulse that threatens

to consume me.

THIS IS NOT A POEM

Just as Jacob
wrestled with an angel,
so do my thoughts
with my prayers.

Words once flowing from my lips
like sweet honey from the rock,
now harden into stone.
Harnessed, not free—
Choked by images of another
woman's husband who is not mine
to hold.

YOUR TOUCH

When I close my eyes
I can *taste* you
kissing me;
feel my soft brown cheeks warm
under the gentle touch
of your large, fumbling hands.

I imagine you rubbing
my back
my thigh
beneath a table
in a public place.

These visions
make me *quiver*;
cause tingles & moments
of excitement & longing
that shoot through
my body like a flare
across a lonesome sky.

SUMMERTIME

You are a sip
of ice water
on a
        hot
dry
        sultry day.

Your presence quenches
my thirst for difference.
Your voice
        cools me
calms me
        causes me
to exhale.

Your hands fan a breeze
across my body.
        I feel you
feel me
        release.

I float in the liquid that is you
& remember the joys of summer
in cooling down after a day
of hot love.

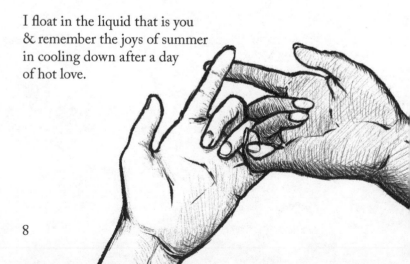

DISCOVERY

I wonder
about these
thoughts of you...

running

rushing

ricocheting

through my mind.

The flow of these musings
arouse my senses & intrude me—
Fever days know no end.

I wonder
what it must be like

to touch your skin

taste your sweat

smell the air

that wreaks of our desire;

to see your reaction
as I whisper
unspoken fantasies.

Such a strange & wonderful
discovery in uncovering
the beauty & potential
of a friendship with you...

MERCURY RISING

There is no
necessity
requirement
or built-in agreement
that our alignment
be more than friendship.

& though the heat
that rises within me
whenever I see you
would send the mercury rising—
I am content
to hold your hand,
share a bottle of wine
over a conversation
that brings both comfort & joy
simply because it promises
the presence of you.

RANDOM THOUGHTS

Random thoughts of you
permeate my private moments
interrupt my rhythm
intrude on my carefully crafted world.

Random thoughts of you
transform my mind's mundane conversations
into interesting chatter—
Words uncertain & unfamiliar.

These thoughts pull me into
fantasy & wonder,
dreaming what it would be like to:

      feel you

          have you

             take me

to the forbidden places
that exist only in my mind.

A place not even safe to discuss
during a private conversation with

myself.

PERMISSION

YOU,
yes you, excite me.
Thoughts of you
interrupt my day & send my mind
on unscheduled vacations.

It's quite a challenge, you should know,
for me to continue
with the mundane & the trivial,
when visions of you
are the competition.

YOU,
yes you, have given me
reason to believe that a woman
should expect to be surprised
by her emotions.

YOU,
yes you, have caused me to smile
when nary a joke has been told;
to lick my lips just at the thought
of yours.
To tilt my head & imagine
a midnight sky that doesn't
stain of loneliness.

YOU,
yes you, have awakened
a mighty spirit in me.
& you have done all of this
without the slightest touch
& certainly with no permission
from me.

MIXED EMOTIONS

I am truly
           happy
that you are
           happy
yet, I am also sad
about your
           happiness
for if you
were experiencing
just a little
           unhappiness
then it could open
up an opportunity
for me to experience
           total bliss.

Ian

The Summer of Intent

"He or she who does not turn things topsy-turvy,
who is unhappy at work,
who does not risk certainty for uncertainty,
to thus follow a dream,
those who do not forego sound advice at least once in their lives,
die slowly."
— MARTHA MEDEIROS

INSOMNIA

Lately,
I can't sleep at night.
I lie awake thinking of you,
anticipating the next time
we will share time, air & space.
Wondering if it can possibly be
as amazing as our first encounter—
When one look in your eyes
had me thinking thoughts
that made me want to hide my face.

TO THE WRITER

Thoughts of you satiate me.
Your smile & soothing voice
remind me to exhale.

When I breathe in the air, it is laced
with cravings for your essence:
the smell of your neck,
the taste of the sweat that seeps
from your skin.

You are with me at night.
Visions of you lull me into dreams
that leave me yearning
for a taste of you the morning after.

In my mind, I've committed the greatest of sins—
Having another, after all this time, enter my spaces.
You've visited me countless times
& with open arms,
I welcome you back, again.

In my mind, I've experienced you
as you uncover what has been hidden
deliberately.

In truth & with time, when we come together
it will merely be a moment on the continuum
of satisfaction.
A moment that we've crafted
long before with thoughts & words.

In its purest form, it will be the fading period
on the end of a perfect sentence—
Just before another one
begins.

THE EYE TRILOGY: EanYolandaEncounter

I. 600 DEGREES OF PASSION

In 600 degrees of passion
there is no shade.
Only pure heat & the lingering
sweet smell of sweat that seeps
through our pores, running down like rain.
Silver stars glistening, bringing joy
like the noonday sun.

In 600 degrees of passion
there is potential for memory to lapse.
Moments of temporary insanity,
minutes & hours feverishly lost
in wonderings & wanderings of the soul.
There are smiles that speak sincerity
through succulent lips that drip
whispered confessions, questioning,
How did we get here. . . so quickly?

In 600 degrees of passion
there is no shade.
No place to retreat.
We come face to face with desire & might—
The unknowing & the hopeful.
In 600 degrees of passion there is the chance
that anything can happen.

II. REQUESTS

You say, *These are my requests for now,*
but what will you ask of me later?
Will I be able to give you what you seek?
Completely? Undeniably?
Deliver all that you wish for?

Will I be able to make you understand
that entrance into my world
is through the other doors that you've stumbled
into, & not the one that you suspected?

Will you believe me when I say
that this encounter is the first
of its kind in nearly four decades
of a life that I, for so long,
considered complete?

Will you be prepared to accept this
for what it is, what it can be,
& someday, what it was?

Can we embrace this feeling
of the tide rushing towards us
while relishing the sweetness of days passed
& expectation of those to come?
Taking it one tender moment at a time?

These are my requests
for now.

III. STRUGGLES

We experienced a moment that was both
unexpected & timely; puzzling yet precise.
An instance that has left an indelible
footprint of longing.

We created touch that seared the skin
through the movement of fingertips
that traveled many miles; strokes that reawaken
memories long forgotten, visiting places unreachable
by those who know & love us.

We reacquainted ourselves with desire & pleasure—
Old friends! They invited us to a party, a celebration
in remembrance of what it feels like to be alive!

We shared gentle moments that reawakened the poetic,
finding strength in each other's spaces;
meeting lines but never crossing them.

We discovered a friendship, a new way of seeing.
Charting the course of a journey that has no map
nor needs one. Setting out on a venture
of what can be; what was then.
Knowing all too well that this moment
occurred long before we ever even met.

QUIET TRICKS

You fill the noisy spaces in my life
with a beautiful silence.
A stillness that is
      tangible
palpable
      palatable
& soothing to my soul.

You are the quiet that I turn to
      throughout the day & night,
      pulling me into welcoming spaces
      & captivating moments.

You are my Houdini.
Your magic transports me
to places known to few,
explored by no one.

Everyone could use a little magic
in their lives; moments when
the heart & mind are moved
while the body stands still,
suspended in time.

INTERESTS

I am interested in you.
I want to caress you, explore you
from the start of your universe
to the end of mine.

I want to discover you
& expose unknown
tenderness.

My interests are simple:
        to sit in silence with you
        to have our bodies touch
        to find the place
where the soul can wonder,
lips can wander
& then there is rest.

I want to
        absorb your words
        breathe your air
        take in the energy you release
& offer moments that make you
smile from deep within—

A smile that no camera can capture;
one only we can understand.

ALAS, THE TIDE (OF WORDS)

like the tide,

there is ebb & flow

in life & in love.

5:59pm

> We seek deeper meaning
> in the eyes of others & long
> for completeness in another's embrace.

6:20pm

sometimes, the healing

is not in the touching...

6:20pm

> But in the words of another.

7:22pm

words...

carefully

thoughtfully

lovingly

chosen to express kindness

& breathe belief into a life

strangled by...

9:16pm

Responsibilities...

9:22pm

realities,

ways of knowing.

9:46

Words that break what seeks
to deplete happiness...

10:07pm

& hold hostage desires.

10:46pm

Like the tides, we have ebbed & flowed
in our love.

11:11pm

✓ Seen, 11:11pm

Angel

Playing House

"Love doesn't just sit there, like a stone, it has to be made, like bread; remade all the time, made new."
— Ursula K. Le Guin
The Lathe of Heaven

WE WERE CHILDREN

Not even our bodies
were fully formed.

I was barely fifteen; you all of nineteen.
There you stood in your manhood,

      young

          underdeveloped

            proud.

& I appeared to you
in my blossoming girlhood,
doused with girlish ways & big dreams.

The gravity of piano keys & percussion notes
pulled us towards one another.
I admired the way you looked, smiled,
& was fascinated by the way you barely
even noticed me.

I knew that you would be my husband
but did not know how.
I knew, even before I understood
what marriage was, that we would be wedded,
together forever.

The years ticked by:
        5. . .10. . .15. . .20. . .25. . .
& during that time

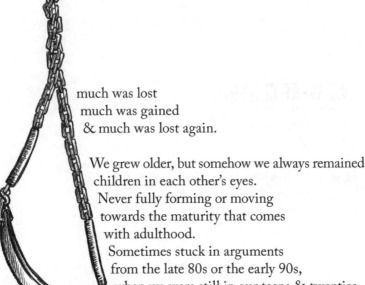

much was lost
 much was gained
  & much was lost again.

 We grew older, but somehow we always remained
  children in each other's eyes.
   Never fully forming or moving
    towards the maturity that comes
    with adulthood.
     Sometimes stuck in arguments
      from the late 80s or the early 90s,
       when we were still in our teens & twenties,
        holding on to what had not been resolved.
         Somehow, never being able to find the

     courage

          understanding

              intellect

to solve our problems in the present or the past.

We were children in so many ways,
we didn't know any better—
We only knew what was in front of us.
We only knew that we tried to overcome:
the brokenness in our families & the racism
of a society that looked at us & scowled.

We only knew how to just be with each other
in the moments that we were together.
When storms hit we didn't quite understand

how to manage.
Attacking each other, blaming each other,
doing what children do on the playground:
throwing sand in each other's faces,
sticking out our tongues & running away.

In some ways it was unfair
that we met so early, I think.
In another lifetime we could have been
best friends, soul mates.
In another lifetime, forever could have been realized.
But so much has happened in our time together,
connected to our formative years—
So much that we didn't have language for,
so much we just couldn't understand—
So we cried or we yelled through it
until we got to the other side.
Only to realize that we
had nothing to hold us
together.

A MOMENT OF REMEMBERING
WHAT LIBERATION FEELS LIKE. . .

At 15 you were the moon & stars—
An image so bright, I could hardly look
at you.

Darkness dissipated & I learned
that life would be good, filled with struggle,
a good struggle, the kind that, together,
we would take on to the finish.

& struggle we did.

The loss of three,
those we desperately wanted
to carry on our name
& the love we found.
Moments of beauty turned into
years of bliss, smiles from deep within—
& even in moments of extreme challenge,
with the loss of the only one
who, besides me, could love you deeply,
we somehow made it through.

Along the way, my desire for

   knowledge

    truth

     movement

made you

uncomfortable

unsettled

unsure

that I wasn't trying to interrupt
what we had created, carved out
just for ourselves.
I intended to preserve that part of our lives,
protect it;
my heart's desire was to expand it…

More for me.

Meant more for *you*.

Then something shifted.

Moments of intimacy, if I am honest,
became work; a means to an end.
A service to cure your anxiety.

A way to

serve

be compliant

& remember

that my body was an offering.
In your temple, it lost meaning for me.

& when the other losses came

year

. . .after year

. . .after year

you told me, *Well it wasn't a real baby anyway*
& I realized that I didn't know you anymore.

But the women in my life saved me.

They gave me hope that even if I
could not bear a child, I was a woman
to be

respected

loved

cared for

believed in.

I had purpose beyond motherhood & wifehood.
& this quest I began.

The beginning of my liberation
meant the end of our journey.

Yes, I came to understand
that you were, in fact,
part of my journey
but not my destination.

For a decade, I sat in the silence of wanting more.
I moved forward with dreams & goals
meaning I moved away from the world
in which you lived & protected.
But somehow, we still slipped
back into each other's orbits;
coming together only to fall apart.

& then *she* came into existence.

My reaction surprised me.

My tears were not those of joy, but of anticipation
for perhaps

       another loss

            another affirmation of my lack
            of womanness

               my inability to provide

the ultimate offering to the universe.

& then she:

Arrived.

Survived.

Blossomed.

We thought we had reached the PromiseLand.
She would take us back to that original moment of innocence
when a kiss was enough to make my heart pound louder
than a symphony of ten African drums.

With all of her beauty came challenges, shifting sands;
my need for grace & your need for forgiveness
for being jealous of your child,
mad at me for deeply loving what we both had longed for,
for so very long.

These things are never intentional.
We are only, & always human.
& at times that is

     ugly

          ragged around the edges

          pitiful.

But I thought that if I loved you more,
showed you my

     superwomaness

          degrees earned

diapers changed

dinners made

that it would save us.
But saving was a stop that we had passed long ago
in places that even the *Kama Sutra*
could not bring us back to.

Others had

entered your spirit

taken your attention

filled you

with the belief that your purpose
was not to be an attentive poppa,
but someone who should seek the simplicity of life—
Recapturing moments before our baby arrived,
living the illusion that we only had each other
to care for in complete bliss.

But I was always the

servant

apology maker

worker

slave,

the one who held it up & together.

But there was now a rip in my cape;
the giving of life had both strengthened
& weakened me.
By the time I discovered where you had been
spending your mind & time, I had nothing left
within me to help preserve the façade that this
would all be okay after a good night's sleep.

& so, I left.

Not physically, like the first time before I returned,
but my heart took a vacation from the space
my body occupied; sending me postcards years later,
refusing to return home.

Then I swayed.

& I knew that the protection I had under

    God

        Christ

            The Spirit

had been compromised.
I sought joy in another place
that only filled me with guilt.
But here we were, trying to travel three roads,
separate ones of our own,
& a single one where we were to be the parents

we thought we had

believed we had

wished we had.

Having moments of success
but mostly moments of disappointment
at our lack of perfection
even though it appeared to others that we
were indeed the perfect couple.

The day I saw the email was one
that knocked the wind out of me.

& your reaction

your breakdown

my breaking through

left what would be the mark of our future.
One where we could not be together
unless trust could be re-established.

But soon, your anxiety would complicate
all that we knew
& challenge my existence as

wife

mother

woman.

One who had her own desires
& tried to find a way
to balance it all.

The beam broke.

The balance lost.

& we entered the next stage,
a transition into the unknowing.

Drunkenness from broken dreams & alcohol corrupted
the journey. Verbal violence & moments of pre-domestic
madness captured in the twilight zone;
moments that helped me to realize that I must break free.
That my freedom was inextricably linked to your need
to keep me caged into the role that I
had played for over two decades.
To be free, I had to seek liberation of my soul
& this is what I have been doing
in the four years that I
have been physically gone
from the space that we shared.

I was in debt, but I am free.

I was alone, but I am free.

I needed help, but I am now free enough to know.

I ripped the tattered cape from my neck—
It fell from my body;
my armor that had kept me both strong & weak,

preserving & disintegrating me
at the same time.

Salvador

The Sabbatical

"You can only coax someone into the vortex
from in the vortex"
—ESTHER HICKS

THE MOVEMENT OF ME

I have changed.
There is no possible way
I can remain the same
after sharing time & space
with you.

Never in my life's history
have I experienced

    the meshing of worlds

        the colliding of spirits

           the depth of reaching

into another's galaxy
while (re)shaping the definition
of my own.

Realizing that making known this shift
takes absolute grace & courage,
all of which, I have learned, I have in abundance.
There was an absolute beauty in my discomfort
of having my mind occupied by a stranger,
who, in record-breaking time, has become more
familiar to me than people I have known
all my life.

This field, this harvest of green
that I have discovered, a place that continues
to be life-giving, requires that I pause to ask:

Yolanda, now exactly what have you learned?

To this I respond:

I have learned what it means to love another
while loving myself even more.
I have learned to dissect experiences
& extract elements that cause me
pain & unhappiness.

I have learned to find my voice, speaking back
to those who have silenced me with my own kindness.
I have learned that I can walk with another,
hold a hand, feel deeply, & truly want for them
the happiness & peace I want for myself,
all while expecting nothing in return—
Except the promise of a better & stronger me,
a better & stronger them,
in this less than perfect world.

I have learned that I am a good friend,
one, who with delight, will pay forward the blessings
she has received from these moments
that cannot be easily described or found
in a book; completely off the page—
Unscripted.

> *I have learned desire.*

I have learned that I can interrupt myself
& not be the person who

shuts down

shuts off

& walks away

when this is exactly what my heart tells me to do.

Run, my heart says. *Leave.*

Take the lowest dosage of pain while it is still available.
I have learned to listen to more than my heart
because at times the heart deceives.
It lies because it has to.

I have learned forgiveness.

I have learned that a true friendship means
there is support of self & the other;
not always simultaneous, not always equally
reciprocal, but always timely
& present when needed.

I have learned happiness.

I have learned that I can be critical of myself
& still be good to myself.

I have learned that it is okay to be passionate—
intense even—to go into the deep spaces of my mind
& publically entertain chatter
instead of holding it within.

I have learned to exhale.

I have learned that I can travel time,
return from time & recognize
that I have gained the insight about the world
that I needed to build for my survival.
Turning inward, communicating
with the libido at the worthy expense
of the cognitive.
I have learned to watch time stand still.

Emotions rule when time is altered.
I learned that first-hand.

I have learned peace.

I have learned that I am a farmer.
That I enjoy the idea of tilling this land
of growth & maturity for seasons to come.
Even when storms hit & crops are threatened,
I will harvest.
I will tend to the land of me
because I have learned
that I am worthy.

A GIFT FROM THE UNIVERSE

You. Me. We.
Travelers on an unexpected trip
into (re)knowing the unknown differently.
Individually, collectively
we travelled old & new territory.
Traversing boundaries set long ago.
On this journey of emancipation & (re)discovery
we met ourselves; people we've always known,
but somehow lost contact with over time.

Sleepless nights that drained & invigorated.
Darkness stretched into light with each new sunrise.
Emotions tested & tried on for size,
at times trying to force what did not fit
out of fear, only to realize that fear
had no welcome mat at our door.

Honesty:

    brutal.

      hurtful.

        liberating.

In service only of:

Revelation.

Healing.

Renewal.

Honesty:

taken.

swallowed like a bitter pill.

medicine chosen & self-prescribed.

Secrets. Hopes. Desires.

Fears coded in language dripped from our lips.
All was open & available for consumption.
Baring souls while chanting incantations;
murmuring prayers & meditations on vulnerability.
Exorcising arrogance cleared the path
for humility & tenderness—
The birth of a true friendship.

A gift from the Universe.

Packaged in past regrets & future hopes.
The promise of revealing the full-version of selves
only to realize they could not be written with certainty.
Because full-selves are always in the making;
chapters continue to be revised,

whole books appearing with the arrival
of a Facebook message after a trip to the future.

A gift to the Universe:

This friendship once again
found itself giving.

     Providing

Preparing

     Nurturing

Knowing

     Anticipating

the hourglass moment
we knew would arrive.
It is here.
& we welcome it.

TODAY

Today, I placed my heart
in a little box
& tucked it away.
I hid it from any feelings & emotions
that would interrupt its peace.

Inside the box were memories—
Moments shared...smiles.

Today, was the first time
I hesitated to ask you how you were.
How your therapy had gone,
how you passed your day.
With this space has come
new territory & what was once
familiar is now strange.

Today was the first time
I saw you but could not recognize you.
I was careful not to trespass the places
I once travelled to with unrestricted access.

Today, I wrapped up
all that gave me joy, like
Christmas
Kwanzaa
Three Kings Day
rolled into a twister of
goodbye.

Today, the Universe returned;
it took back the friendship
it had once given.

I mourned twice today.
First, for what could have never been
& then for what had passed.

Zaren

Crisis of Interruption

"The biggest coward of a man is to awaken the love of a woman without the intention of loving her."
—Bob Marley

WHAT I KNOW TO BE TRUE

As B follows A in the alphabet
& night follows day with an evening sunset,
I could not be more clear in how I feel about you.

As all of my friends tell me to run—
They know healing a broken heart
is never fun.
I could not be more clear
about how you make me feel.

As thoughts swarm my head that you
are too good to be true
& your treatment of my heart
gives me more than a clue,
I, still in all of this, could not be more clear
about my feelings for you.

This is the foolishness of love songs.
The *stuff* of emotions that scare.

These are the feelings that, I'm sure,
make me appear a lot less sane
than I am.

How can I claim to love someone
I barely know?
Knowing barely more
than your name.
This ride intrigues & exhausts me.

It steadily reminds me
that to be alive as my FULL self
is to take risks, & by choice, ignore
all the signs that will someday
make me wish I had never met you.

THE WEEKEND

(On the Occasion of Yolie's 48th Birthday)

That weekend you saved my life.
You held the night in your hands,
allowed me to choose the stars
that gave me pleasure
& sprinkled me with their delight.

You moved me to places I had yet
to discover & smiled when you wished for

      the twilight

        the dawn

            the morning dew
to appear.

The night & day obeyed you.
I, too, was under your command.

That weekend, you claimed my life.
My future suddenly included you.
You, the nexus that sprouted in less
than 24 hours, commanded me to dream
of new birth, beginnings with only continuations,
& a life yet to be.
The crash came only days after
when I realized it was *just a weekend*.

A weekend of fantasy & fiction,
longing & need.
But now, I harken back to a time
when I was awake.

Wide awake.

Terror struck.

Trauma reentered.

All possibility faded to black—
Back before the weekend began.
While the world was turning,
I disconnected all possibilities
of others. Sending messages & giving
in-person soliloquies about how you,
Zaren, let me hold the universe in my hands
while I fell in love with you.

Reality is a bitter pill to swallow
but as I am life's patient,
I understand that with every risk at love,
there is pain & I have my fair share
of dosage to take.

& through this, I will live.
I will love, yet again.
This too, in time,
shall pass.

THE APPEARANCE OF YOU

Since you've entered my world
there isn't a day that returns to night
that I don't think of you.

Your face, a warm smile
that greets me when I open my eyes.
When you are near, your smell, your voice
fill all that is around me in ways that give
me life, & take my breath away
in an instant.

You have caused me to feel again.
You make me want to imagine what it means
to let someone in & dream in the colorful ways
of my past.

You have caused me to question:

*Has there ever been a time
that I've been held in the way you
hold me?*

      Stroked.

        Touched.

            Entered into depths

that I did not know existed.

You've caught me by surprise
& I am in awe of myself & of the you
who has appeared.

Where did you come from?

    When did you arrive?

Who gave you permission

    to greet my heart;

      embrace my soul;

        enter my mind;

find rest within the space of me?

You smell of peace.
You taste of joy.
Your sound is calm & chaos
all at once.

A bold release of tension
held tight in the body,
appearing only when the signal
of desire has sounded—
I hear it & I sing its beauty.
I welcome its song & open myself to it: *Love*.

A HAIKU ON RISK

Zaren, you opened your mouth
& without thinking
I opened my heart.

ON PAIN & JOY WITH/IN LOVE

This is less about my insecurity
& more about your desire
to tame how Love flows.
But if you know anything,
you know that Love
cannot be controlled.

Love goes where it chooses —
oftentimes it is not

      welcomed

         desired

            needed...

but yet it appears.

Love does not wait for an invitation
or a more convenient time,
like when a daughter grows older.

Love interrupts at the most
inconvenient times, reminding us
that it is, & has always been, in control
of when & where it enters.

Your heart can protest,
but if it is real Love,
it will not matter.

We are mortal & limited.
If we didn't pretend to have control,
we would wander this life
at the beck & call of Love.

Love is merciless at times & yet it is

  patient

   kind

     & sometimes compromising;

indulging the childish ways of the heart.

At times, love helps us to see
how much in need of it we are.
It shows us sympathy, empathy even,
especially for those of us

who most pathetically cannot resist
its power.

Why do I love thee?
I haven't a clue!
You appeared unexpectedly
though I have prayed for you all my life,
or at least for what I thought
you could represent:

Someone who would finally
love me in a way that I deserve.

Someone to hold me & tell me
that everything will be alright
at the

      moment

         tonight

            & in the morning.

Someone who is not afraid
to tell me that they love me
in the way that I love them:

      without limits

         openly

            frighteningly free.

Someone who is not afraid of my heart—or theirs.

Someone who recognizes a heart like mine,
open & willing to give & receive
in ways not known to Wo/man.

I believe in the *idea* of love.

I believe in the *power* of love.

I believe in the *pain* that real love brings
when it is unrequited, & the *joy* that comes
when it is reciprocated.

Living for Love itself
is how I have chosen to love
in this lifetime.

MISSING YOU

Edna St. Vincent Millay said
that if you are missing someone,
it is likely that they are missing you, too.

I talked to the Gods & They
understand & agree there is no way
you can miss me more than I miss

the stretch of your smile

   the warmth of your eyes

the feel of your touch

   the essence of you.

It is not possible for you
to long for me in ways I do for

   the smell of your neck

      the taste of your skin

        the melodious sound of your voice.

The Gods have met & They all agree
that when it comes to missing you,
no other body compares to the way
mine curves at the whisper of your name.
My spine curls & my very being
sings praises to your holiness.

My only relief is to comfort myself
& recall the motions of your embrace.

This distance in miles, this time,
cannot be overcome, it seems.
It is almost impossible to wait
& exercise the patience you ask of me.

Time is the enemy & distance a demon,
in this love affair that sparked a fortnight ago
but has changed me forever.

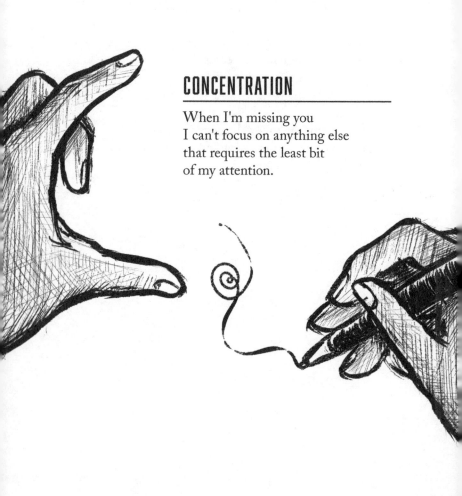

CONCENTRATION

When I'm missing you
I can't focus on anything else
that requires the least bit
of my attention.

TEA WITH GOD

I learned early on in my spiritual life
never to question God.
But lately, I've felt the impulse
to sit for tea with God & ask a few questions:

> *Why on Earth did You have me*
> *fall in love with a man*
> *who lives in a city*
> *I have always despised?*
> *A man whose career*
> *has only caused surges*
> *of hate within me?*
>
> *Why would You allow my heart*
> *to be unlocked by someone, who, on the surface,*
> *doesn't seem to give a shit about being*
> *in a relationship with me?*

What is my lesson here?
Is this a rhetorical exercise?
Or a quest for me to find an answer
to the perennial question
elegantly & eloquently posed by the
1950s philosopher Frankie Lymon:

> *Why do fools fall in love?*

I am a fool.

I have allowed myself to slip heart first
into a breathing space where I have not
checked the air pressure or the quality.

I am the fool who has allowed God
to let my heart be open to words
that I've longed to hear coming from the lips
of someone whose reflection
mirrors my own.

I am the fool who has fallen
for a person who understands the struggle
in ways that I do & never can,
who can hold me closely &

  whisper

    rant

      rage

against the machine that is this

  broken

    beaten

      battered

falsity of a democratic nation.
Who can then release the pressure
that is the work of our blackness.

Blackness matters to me in life & in love.
My heart knew this long before my body did.
Yet, my body knew this all along.
My spiritual godparents—Jimmy, Malcolm, Toni—
speak through me each time I write
to & about the cop in Boston,
who finds it challenging to communicate with me—
Except when his body speaks to mine.
In those moments we share the same

       tongue

          language

             love

interlocking intimately, dizzying me, dazzling
the spaces around us until we as one
are the most captivating light show
in the darkest parts of 2am.

When his body talks to mine,
all the things that I hate the most
about his profession & that city
evaporate around us, hanging overhead,
thickening the air as it mixes
with his sweat, my hair.

Today, reality has no bearing
on the fact that I have never felt so alive
than that moment in June when I looked

into his eyes & saw a soul that reflects
& intertwines with mine
in a search for love.

Yes, God. We have a few things to talk about.

CLARITY

When everything is clear
& I am beyond certain
that you don't give a damn,
caring becomes a futile act on my part.

LEAVING THE VORTEX

My passion for you
is no longer useful
now that you know
my potential
to love you.

I will not slip again into sadness.
I will not write streams of consciousness
that spiral my heart into the vortex.

I am grateful for the vortex;
it has served me well.
It is now time to leave it behind
& discover what beauty awaits.

TARGET PRACTICE

There you stand
towering over me
both black & blue.
Dark to the night,
yourself, in the most insidious ways.
You are a danger to yourself
& anyone who tries to know you.

Your heart, enclosed
by an electric fence, sends deadly shock waves
through the system of the ones who move

       close

          trespass

             attempt

to understand the intricate world
you have created of

fear

     trauma

vulnerability

     women's tears.

All this makes you feel powerful.

You are

        upstanding

          purposeful

            strong—

A man of your community built on lies & deceit.

You, a music lover, croon empty lyrics
of care, distorted harmonies echoing
faux affection & misrepresentations of love.

You whisper into willing

        ears

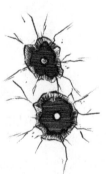

          palms

            parted lips.

Your new song marks them
as collateral damage; new additions
to your museum of pain & hurt.
On display across the bar
or at one of your secret brotherhood meetings,
you parrot the same story, tirelessly, vindicated
You tell how you saved each one from themselves—

This one abused.
That one newly divorced.
The other one jaded by love.

All diagnosed by your closed fists as

     crazy

       stalker

          uninvited.

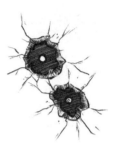

& since you can no longer protect & serve
the streets that you were given
unbridled authority over, you instead walk
the beat of broken hearts.
You destroy & serve,
wound only to protect
after the damage is done.

I can still feel the ring of metal
ricocheting against my chest
threatening to

      pull me in…

        sink me…

          drown me.

THE NECKLACE

Let me block your crazy ass,
Your necklace is in the mail —goodbye!

This is what your penultimate text read.

It's been weeks & I still await the arrival
of the necklace; that blue necklace.
A freudian slip I left behind
during one of those nights I fell in love
with you, again.

But you won't release the necklace.
It has become a

      reminder

         a token

            a symbol

of what this was & what it was not.
Each delicate crystal beam of blue—
The exact feeling that bathed over me
whenever I waited & waited for you to call.

But here's a secret: You will *keep* the necklace.

Remind yourself of how fragile I was,
how easily you had me
in the palm of your hands
& then lost me
through your fingertips.

Our time was not one of love—
It was the illusion of love, the haunting of heartbreak.
To love, one must be willing to be open
to baring vulnerabilities & exposing fear.

You are paid to be brave,
unafraid is the only thing you know.
But tenderness & trust are so foreign to you,
you recoil at their call.

Job. Money. Power.
[is your]
Wife. Mistress. Love.

I wanted nothing more than to love you.
I was willing to be fragile in your presence—
I had hoped you would not take for granted
my semi precious jewels:

Body.

Mind.

Passion.

I am the necklace you flung
into your jewelry box of lovers,
tangling me up in the mess of your habit
of trading precious stone
for the next rock that comes along,
painted as a jewel.

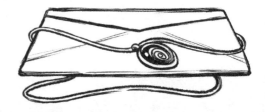

A MEMBER OF THE WEDDING

A year from now I am going to marry you.
You held my face between your hands,
looked directly into my eyes &
spoke a broken promise.

A promise made on a dime, in the heat
of the moment; one you deliberately unraveled
from the moment you thought it.

For eight months you pulled me along for a ride
before running me over.
You ripped open my heart,
left exposed at the side of the road—
nutrition for all of the lonely travelers, heartbreak hitchhikers.

There will be no marriage a year from now.
No crisp invitations, no flowers, no dress.
There is only

      you

          me

               & this empty dream,

swaying between us, daring someone
to open their eyes first.

THE TRUTH IN BLACK & BLUE

The truth is, had you not spoken of Malcolm
in the way that you did,
had you not talked of your father & your love
for him & his love for Malcolm—
I would have made no room
for you.

If you had not been a Black man
I would have never given you any play,
much less let you play
with my heart.

I'm not quite sure why I opened
myself to you.
Given how I feel about those in Blue,
even though you were Black
& Blue—

You were still my choice.

I admit, something positive
has come from this.
My loathing has mellowed—
I faced my own hypocrisy
about loving all humankind,
except those who wear badges.

You challenged this by making me fall
in love with you & the sight of you
in Blue, Black man.

Your blackness overshadowed
your Blue.
But Blue is what I was left feeling
whenever I talked to you.

What's your story?

What can I do for you?

What are you looking for?

I didn't quite know how to answer then.
But now, since things have fallen apart,
I finally have a response:

What's your story?

What were you looking for?

How do you awaken a woman's love,
drag her into your world
& destroy all hope?

How do you reconcile saying things like:

    I love you

        I will marry you

            I love being with you…

Curse her out & then walk away?

Is that something you learned
in police school?
Did they teach you to go all in…
then pull all out, immediately,
without checking for bloodshed or tears?

Where did you learn to treat people
as temporary & disposable?
Why do you fight others when the enemy
is within? I am not the enemy.
I chose to love you.

If you had not been a Black man
I would have never given you any play,
much less let you play with my heart.

The truth is, you were Blue
& that should have stopped me
from the very start.

A HEARTY MEAL

Never offer your heart to a man who eats hearts.
—Alice Walker

You look like you devour hearts for sport.
My heart, unfamiliar to myself, vulnerable to others,
is a perfect target for game.

Listening deeply shows me a window into
your past & present; filled with visions familiar
to those in the vortex that rocked my world.

I am not interested in taking those trips again.
Traveling roads that lead to liberating exhaustion.
I just don't have the bandwidth right now.

Your personality is uncanny. Strange even.
& I wonder if there is an anxiety train you are trying
to catch or run away from, unsure of which stop is yours.

You gather passengers & bystanders along the way.
Eventually, you stop to decide if the ride was
worth it.

I think you would chew my heart up
& spit it out.
Just for sport.
Just because you can.

Drunk with power & the need to control,
I would just be a switch; to be flicked on & off
at your convenience.

A picture; a flash of a smile.
A blow of your horn all to keep me
on the table. A slab of flesh.

The vortex taught me to be leery, especially now,
of my co-pilot.
I have a vacancy in that space & I am not interested
in you returning to fill it.

I want to distance myself from you
in every way possible.
I want to distance myself from the ones
who hurt.

I need to run before my heart is wrecked
beyond recognition.

BLISS IN FLIGHT

I feel light like a bird in flight.

This load has lessened.
Once, carrying for two;
I now feel lighter, freer—
Is it possible to be
one in a relationship?

I have fallen more
in love with myself, releasing
the anchor that was you.

From the start, I made this be
what I knew it could not.
Yet, I desired love.
Held a hunger for it
that demanded to be satiated.
When I looked in your eyes,
I saw warm summer evenings;
the promise of love.

I saw late night train rides,
my head warm within the crook
of your neck.
I saw winter sunsets.
I saw a future with you.

But like the ghosts that sleep
in mirrors or sandcastles too close
to the shore, it all disappeared.

Maybe, it was never there.

We could have laughed.

We could have loved.

We could have been two who shared
what is deepest in one's heart.

We could have been two who shared
memories & talked in a language
that only few understand.
We could have gone into the depths of
our past, terrified but together.

You did not care.

　　　You were not ready.

　　　　　You could not *see* me.

You were not interested.

But now, it is time for release.
It is time for reality.
To face the truth that someone
else had your heart all along.

There is so much darkness in you.
There is so much light in me—

It demanded too much of you:

Your smile.

Your happiness.

Your healing.

But pain is your comfort.
Look how she caresses you, cradles you.

Anger is your lover.
Look how she adores you, makes you feel
like more of a man.

Tyrone

To Ride or Die for Love

"Should I smile because you're my friend,
or cry because that's all you'll ever be?"
—Anonymous

THE LIBRA'S CYCLE OF LOVE

I am fast to fall in love
but slow to remember
how much it hurts
when the love is not
returned.
I am slow to realize
that my heart has been broken
into tiny pieces—
Because as I pick them up,
I have already started
to love someone new,
again.

(UN)COMMITMENT

There are moments when I remember you. When we fit & it felt like I'd known you all of my life...or at least, half of it. There are minutes when I recall your favorite color, the amazing story of how you saved your life & others. In those moments I dream of a life together, where three of us are one. But then I hear a voice that says, "No, she would never really see me as an authority" & then I hear a sound, feel a movement that reminds me: I wasn't their choice. I may never meet the woman you love most or the man you call best friend. It is in those moments & minutes that I feel like a secret—Someone to be hidden, tucked away. I am reminded that I don't really know you. & if that's the case, then I have been loving

a mask

a trick of the light

a cruel, broken promise.

THE WAITING ROOM

I will wait (patiently)
on the love I deserve.
I am going to believe
it can happen.
It will not be a love
that requires work.
This love will

       move when I am still

          speak when I am quiet

             stand when I am falling.

This love will welcome me
with outstretched arms & whisper,

     I have been here,
     (patiently) waiting for you
     & this moment to arrive.

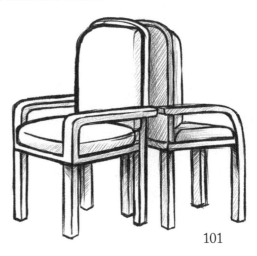

BLACK UNICORNS

I think ours is
a different
kind of love.
One between two unicorns
amongst a sea of stable horses.

Not many, ourselves included,
know to what depth this love
can sink to, rise from.
Are we a single moment, tied together
with a bird's breath?
Or are we a spiral, spinning
into a lifetime?

THE RISK OF LOVE

We have been building
a bond that stretches
nearly two whole years.
This bond is elastic, fragile.
So palpable with
uncertainty.
We are aware it holds the promise
to break the very moment
either one of us decides
to breathe.

TO LOVE A PISCES

I am most insecure
with you.
I am most secure
with you.

My vulnerabilities
explode in your presence—
I am brought to safety.

I am most afraid
with you.
I am most courageous
with you.

My instinct to run
is activated, yet I find rest
in your arms.

Doubt lingers.
Unwanted questions remain.
But I am ever fully present
to accept this is the work of the heart
when it decides to love.

A CHANCE AT LOVE

It is senseless to think
this will be easy.
But, if we follow the paths
where our hearts lead,
we know it can be
possible.

S.E.E. OF LOVE

Now that you have slept
beside me, this bed is an oasis.
I am lost in its reflection
of sound & time; a place of touching
fingertips against the fullness
of lips & thighs.

The warmth of your memory remains.
Etched on

     my sheets

        within my heart

           across my lips.

It is you, in that fleeting
moment, that I will always
remember.

EPIPHANY

I cannot recall a time before this
when my soul was touched
by someone's eyes.

You looked at me
& my heart knew—
It knew that this was a different kind
of being—

Togetherness.

A different stroke of luck,
a new way that all of me
was being invited to be
my liberated self
in the face of Love.

BREAKFAST | TIME

I want to wake up with you.
Share mornings & tea,
capture & hold moments
that keep us close.

I miss you
when I am on the phone
with you & curse the distance
between us.

On those rare occasions
when we are together,
I dread the time when we'll be
apart.

Time is tension.
I desire more of it & wish
it went by quickly,
so that I may breathe you in
& rest in your arms
again.

TRIAGE IN WAITING

To wait
on love
takes patience.

Hearts fill waiting rooms
with incessant chatter—
Questioning old pain
& new hopes.

You wait
in silence
& find

the answers are right there—
within your reach.

SPREAD LOVE

It was only in that moment
of letting you go
that I learned the way to
spread love is to live free.

You embody all that is love.
You promote it in the way you move—
Your swagger speaks of love.

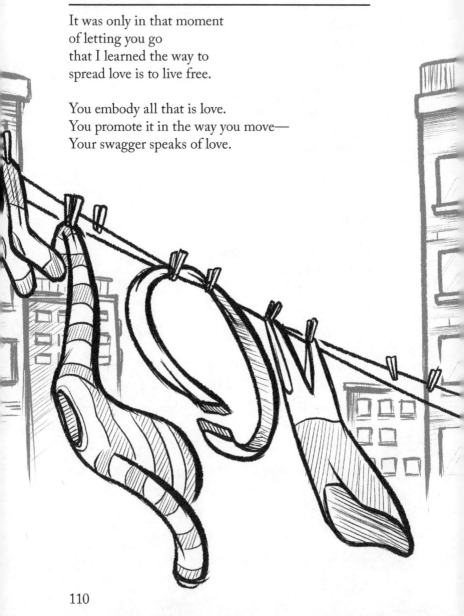

Love is in the warmth of your eyes,
the beauty of your smile.
You carry love in the movement
of your hands.

Even the clothes you wear speak of love.
I hear it, just as my heart did
when we first met.
My heart heard & listened.

Love, I am still
listening.

HER, HIM, YOU & ME

I exist
between a mirror &
a window
when it comes to our love.

I am treating Her the way You
treat me: aloof & nonchalant.
While I have no romantic feelings
for her, I realize the value she brings
to my daughter's life.

I have learned to keep her close,
but at a distance.
I have learned how to do all of this
from You, my most valued teacher.

The mirror she holds allows Me to see
You...Us.
It allows a view into an immediate future
that is

       vacant

          hopeless

             bleh.

Here is the mirror reflecting all
that I have come to know & appreciate about myself;
leaving the wisdom & protection of the vortex,
entering a world of full presence, I embrace that I
am special, kind, beautiful, worthy of a man's

       time

          attention

             love.

I am Queen.

I desire that my man, my partner yet to be,
to both love me & be in love with me—
The temporary & the permanent is what feels right.

Through this window, He passes
words & thoughts most deserving of Me.
As they flow, they are pleasing
to my heart. These words feel fresh, but familiar—
He is speaking to the woman I once knew.

As I am now awaken to the fullness of Me,
I recognize that what You offer
no longer fulfills. In truth, it never did.
But I became accustomed to sacrificing myself for the
joy of others.

Well, dear, it has now come to this:
Until You shine the mirror on yourself & remove
the fog from the window where You view Me,
You may never really see Me.

To see Me may mean You have to see yourself
anew. A new You not yet ready to face
a world of friends & family
from which you seek & need
approval
            grace
love.

My love is not strong enough to make You defiant.
You did not receive the full power of my love
when it was being passed freely & openly
through my window & into your hands.

HARD LOVE

When I choose to love you,
you will know it.
In true Libra fashion,
my love will come fast,
it will come hard,
& it will run deep.

You will not know what hit you,
but, as it is a steady love
you will have time to unwrap it.

Bit by bit,
poco a poco,
you will come to know
that every
poem
text
voice message
is a gift that serves as testimony.

I pray you are a worthy witness—
That in full presence
you can receive the power
of my gift
& respond graciously.

AN EVOLUTION OF LOVE

Here, I wait for you—

Us.

Standing still yet circling
back again to a love
once familiar, now distant.

I hold a tongue that desires
to loosen itself from those
three words.

Words you only know how to perform.

To say them perhaps
breaks the spell or
states the obvious or
signals the next phase in its evolution.

Rising, I am allowing myself
a steadiness when we are together
& apart.

This evolution of stillness brings
a peace I have not yet held.
This quiet love speaks volumes.
I hear it in your eyes—
It is the sweetest song
my heart has ever known.

A PARTING POEM FOR THE BOYS AT THE CABIN

In the morning
I will mourn what could have been.
I will mourn what I believe
could have given me air
in moments that sought to choke
the life out of my hopes &
dreams.

I will mourn the friendship
I thought we had; an embracing
of how we are becoming humans,
how we are finding self,
how we are learning
to love.

I will mourn our friendship &
its restrictions, handcuffs that held us
in places we wanted to escape.

I will release the mourning of you,
let go of what feels like an albatross
hung around my heart.

I will release the sadness of hurt
that is home-like in its familiarity,
necessary to get through
this life, whole.

Wholeness seems solid—
A feeling, concept.
Completeness is a fairy—
A tale that moves stories
along.

I seek to live in reality.
I want my love & peace
in moments that remind me:

I am alive
I desire to live
& must go after this life
with my eyes & heart wide open.

FULL PRESENCE

You make me
      remember
that life
      is the one thing
I cannot
      forget to
live.

WEEKLY FRIEND IN A BOX

Your *good mornings* are riveting—
Ricocheting shrills that call out my name
& come to me like clockwork:

after 10 & always before noon.

On Mondays you open me, marvelously.
On Tuesdays you tell me all that I am, deliciously
On Wednesdays you make me believe the future
is for us.

Is this what it means for fools to feast?

I, too, am thankful for the Thursdays
that are honest & revealing—
Bringing me closer to reality
& reminding me that love,
the true kind,
must be reciprocal, on any day,
but especially on Fridays—
Where you take the liberty
to put me into your friend box,
& tuck me away until Monday,
when you recycle your process
of (dis)illusion all over again.

COMMITMENT

I know that I am ready
to love you
because I am prepared
to lose you.

MOTORCYCLE RAIN

Your love is like the rain;
it cleanses me.
Your water clarifies the work of the sun—
& the sun always returns.

Your love is a breeze across my heart.
In subtle & tender moments it flutters
my butterfly soul.

FOLLOW THE SUN

It takes patience & courage to choose—
I choose to walk with uncertainty
through ambiguity;
maintaining my dignity & belief
that we were meant to be.

Meant to walk this journey together,
a search for momentum that carries the risk
only an open heart can hold
when love is the choice.

I am not Catholic, but I confess:

It is you.

I knew it was you the moment
we exchanged smiles.
It has always been you without
much resistance from me.

But I feel your trepidation, like
        the heat that prickles my skin
the bird reluctant to leave the egg
        the toddler learning to walk,
one step forward, two back & a fall—

I have fallen for you.

Yet, remain a witness to
your wonderings about me.
Still I offer you this invitation to love
yourself & me.

I sit with patience—
In fellowship we have become good friends.
I invite you to meet with us
as we make space to recognize
the gift of having met.

I have broken through fear today.
I have wrestled with my thoughts
as fear tugged at my heart.
Found the courage to say
what I always knew to be true:

I. Choose. You.

I hope you accept this invitation
& choose to be fully present
when my heart arrives for a visit.
I hope you choose to be courageous
in moments of fear,
delimit the possibilities
to consider that this could in fact
be a beautiful friendship.

I hope you choose to build
a different kind of family
with me.

Us. Together. As one.

Show me your fears,
your scars.
Tell me what is in
your heart; I promise

I will not walk away.

This invitation calls for
patience & courage,
both of which I have in abundance.
So why not just talk?
Let's just talk & see where it goes.
If we end up in a place we don't want to be,
we can just turn around
& follow the sun.

BAGGAGE

You carry the story in your eyes—
It weighs on your shoulders.

There are days you swallow
it whole—
But on the rare occasions
when you set it free,
those of us who listen & hear
are blessed & made all
        the
              more
                    wiser.

I WANT

For the past two years I've been having
a conversation with myself that goes
something like this:

> *Yolie, you have to teach someone*
> *how to love you. You have to know what you need*
> *& believe that you are deserving of the love*
> *you desire.*

Never have I felt the passion of these words
more than the moments that I spend with you.
Months seem like minutes
& minutes are never enough when I
am in the presence of you.

Your boldness to share what you want
has inspired me to write my own list of desires.
Unafraid with a refusal to be shamed,
I admit that:

I want someone to love me in an R&B love song kind of way.
I want someone to hold my hand when the cold
wraps me up in an icy sweater,
&, on the hottest day of the year,
I want someone's eyes to spark
at the sight of mine, like I'm the greatest
light show in July.
I want someone to smile
as wide as the Grand Canyon
when I call or text.

I want someone worth seeing the Grand Canyon with.
I want someone who goes to the Grand Canyon
with me but still thinks I'm the best view.
I want someone to think of me

    morning

        noon

           & night.

I want someone to think of me
when they see another couple
holding hands, the sun caressing their faces.
I want someone to miss me.
I want someone who hits me up
on the daily, first, always a good morning
text & a how-was-your-day phone call
when they can't make it in person.
I want someone to touch me in places
that I am too shy to ask.
I want someone that I can trust all
of the private spaces on my body with,
all the private places in my mind, my soul.
I want someone to kiss me into high
vibrations, transform my mood & make me
close my eyes at the very thought of his soft lips on mine.
I want someone to

    cry with

        laugh with

do with

be with.

I want someone to unzip my dress at the end of the night,
to slip off my heels, to come undone with.
I want someone to hold, to whisper things
only the impulsive me says;
without control, without judgement, only with ease.
I want someone to embrace my togetherness,
my stick-to-it-ness.
I want someone to want me just as much as I want him;
not more, not less, but in a way that is

even

balanced

limitless.

I want someone who will not run,
who will hold my love with care & say,
Thank you for trusting me with this.

WHEN WORDS FAIL

I know no other way to speak to your heart
than through the words that I write in free form—
Words written to say what I cannot,
words that become trapped under my tongue
whenever I look at you.

Contemplation gives me the eerie feeling
that we have both been here before. A
place where joy & happiness dance
with fear & sorrow,
longing & uncertainty.

I want to run. I want to turn away
before you hurt me first.
& I think I will.
It is what I have learned
to do to survive.
It is painful, but I am good at what I do.
I want to spare what I anticipate
is coming; if not now, then tomorrow,
or five years from now.
Time is illusive when the inevitable is at hand.
My heart is much too weak for this.

Love is a strange thing.
We desire it.
We describe how we wish to experience it;
convince ourselves we are ready
& open for it.

It happens every time.

I open my heart with purity
& find myself alone, abandoned & mangled,
wondering to myself: *Why do I bother to love?*

SEMI-PRESENT

Every few days or so
you slip into a vortex
& disappear.
On this end, I wonder:
Where have you been?
With whom?
Have you met them or yourself
in the place you go to
   cry
laugh
   & just be?

& just as I decide to
pull away & enter absence,
you reappear.
I hear your smile
& slightly, but
never completely,
start loving you
again.

A GOODBYE IN THE MAKING

Today, I mourned what was & what could
never be between us.

I mourned

    your smile

        your touch

            memories filled with joy & laughter.

I mourned the moments that were
fleeting, unable to be fully captured
because I was still in a dream state
when I met you.
My heart cried over all the untold stories
you insist are not secrets,
the moments I will never share with you
as you unravel to find
yourself.

Today I was real with myself.
I talked to myself in languages not of

    manipulation

      hope

        despair.

I spoke to myself in tongues of equanimity.
My two selves discussed how *you & I*
simply missed each other this time around—
Traveling different paths because the orbit
of our journeys required us to do so...

& I am saddened by all of this.

Steadily, I anticipate the relief that will come
when my tears dry, when I finally release the pain
from imagining you in the arms of another,
telling your stories & dreaming.

Today, I questioned why I opened my heart to you
& continued to believe in love.
The answer is one that I know:

I have to love.

I *want* to love.

I love amidst the pain
because the pain liberates me,
reminds me of my will to survive.
Love cradles me, a newborn, still exploring
her heart's surroundings;
crawling low, aiming high,
wanting to be held & caressed.

I wonder where the other is,
the one who is not afraid to commit
to a love that keeps one up at night
& makes one think of someone

at the fresh smell of morning dew—
This is what my heart mourned today.

I lay frozen in a state of vulnerability,
but this stillness is progress from the lies
I've told myself.
Lies I want to tell others
about me not loving you.
I feel powerless in the face of a heart interrupted—
One that wants to speak in a language unrecognized
by the men who have stood before me.

Today, I finally began to let go...again.
I've released hope that in this lifetime
we could figure out what it means to be together,
what it means to defy the odds.

I will bury my hope with the

     journals

        poems

           letters.

Artifacts of my
unreconciled & inconsolable
pain.

MUSEUM OF TRIED

You are now a relic
which stands in my
museum of lost loves.
God knows I tried to love you,
tried to help you see that the
world you choose to exist in
is one of many & not
the only one.

I tried to be a good friend
even when you were not one to me.
Even as you kept me tucked away
for easy access.
& with a pure heart, I complied.

I tried not to burden you
so I kept thoughts to myself,
only to realize that my silence
could not protect me.

Family

Friends

God Herself

told me about my silence,
but I did not listen.
I went vipassana on my emotions;
keeping my observations & thoughts
to myself for my safety…& yours.

My familiar became strange;
often finding myself looking twice
just to be sure of what
I was seeing; praying three times
just to understand what I was feeling.
I started collecting
pieces of me & my broken heart;
placed them on display
in letters & poetry for you & all
of the world to see.

You complete my latest exhibition:

Fantasies & Hopes for Reciprocal Love.
Here, in my Museum of Tried,
my tired soul & heart find rest.

Here is where memories of you & your laughter,

       the pain

joy

       confusion

of the past 26 months
will remain.

I will visit them only in brave moments
when I find the courage to face
what happened on the day I decided
to believe in love again.

STRENGTH

I feel strong today.

Strong, like I can scale a skyscraper,
move a mountain into the sea.
Strong, like finally my strength has allowed
me to sit with Reality & commune with her.

Today, I accepted that I was the one
who kept the game going—
It was my love that made
it all possible.

& I am not afraid to embrace my truth,
not afraid to let you go
as I face what never was
or could be.

I have played the major & minor
roles in this play about a love
I would never have with you.
Today, again, I interrupted myself
& finally,

I

        feel

                free.

Other Poems

Who experiences the vortex and lives to tell about it?
The Writer.
—Yolanda Sealey-Ruiz

ICARUS

If only I could transport
myself into your arms
when you needed to hold me.
I would try to be held.

The distance between us
sometimes feels unbearable,
too much to handle after a day
in the life that requires all
of me.

Your arms are respite.
Your eyes peace-like.

The sound of a babbling brook
lullabying me into slumber.
You are a ray of sunshine
that I would offer my wings to.

TODAY, AGAIN

At just the sight of you
I thought about
the wonderful possibilities
that life can offer.

Your smell, your smile
reminded me of why it is
so great to be alive.

THE BRONX, CIRCA 1983

I am always thinking of that place/
the hood that nurtured me & helped
to shape me into the woman/
I am...& becoming.

I have always held you
close/
wrapped in my arms
of blazing fire & ashes/
I knew you before you knew
yourself/
I saved you when others
wanted to throw you/
back to ashes
from which you rose/
like a Phoenix you came
rising & rushing/
towards the midnight sky.

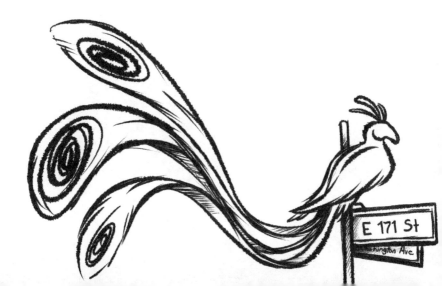

E 171 St

...hington Ave

THE LESSON

You are cautious with
my power.
You know that I can see you,
feel you in ways that shake your
soul.

When you entered
I thought you had come
to stay.
I now see you were only meant
to visit until my work was done.

LIFE

The uncertainty that lies before me
makes me wonder if this is really
what life is all about?
Living in spaces of discomfort,
teetering between the known & unknown,
the unrecognizable & the familiar,
trying to make sense of it all.
It's tiring, I admit it.

The

        hustle

           game

              run

                  mystery.

But if I knew all the answers, the outcomes,
would I still think life to be
as exciting?
Would the disappointments be
as abysmal & the victories
as sweet?

MECCA

We all desire a private
Mecca.
The journey which represents
our sanctified possession
of truth.

Our proof that we have
strayed, erred, but somehow
returned to Love.

SENSATIONS

I admit it—
I still think of you often.
I see you as you stare
deep into my eyes
in gentle & loving wayz.

I am ashamed by my titillation
from the fantasy
& turn away from mirrors;
I cannot stand to see
what you have done to me.

I can't explain how this image
energizes & drains me
at the same time,
how badly I want
to hold you & smother my face
against the flesh between the curve
of your shoulders & neck,
if only for one night.

SEASONAL

I break out
in hives
when my body isn't
next to yours.

I am allergic to
the absence
of you.

THE AWAKENING

Equanimity is peace.
Between light & darkness
lies pain & pleasure.
I approach it all through
the art of living & dying
& living again.

JUST US

Here is my invitation
for you to bend towards
justice.
My arc of self bends
in favor of love—

Asking hard questions
& waiting for answers
that don't offer conclusions,
just more wonderings
about how to live a life
worthy of the children
who come after us.

ABOUT TIME

I feel like time
is running away
from me.
I now know
the only way
to catch it,
is to sit

absolutely

still.

NIGHT & DAY

One lover says,

>   *We should be together in the dark.*

Another lover says,

>   *Welcome to the light.*

His light beckons me, calls me to places
that I have never been.
Places I recognize only in my

>   dreams

>   hopes

>   future

during seasons of love.

One lover says,

>   *I won't tell you about your power.*

Another lover says,

>   *Your power is Awesome.*

We both recognize that humans
have superpowers in the face of love.
A super powerful

emotion

reaction

force of nature

that changes the World & her people.

One lover says,

When I touch you, you will be sure to cry from pleasure.

Another lover says nothing at all,
but holds me in a way that brings tears
to my eyes; tears that cleanse my soul
& washes away past hurt.
Water falling, clearing a path
for this new journey
we both are walking.

One lover says,

I am the greatest you will ever love.

Another lover says,

You are great & I am grateful.

& it is this love that I am drawn to & thankful for.

It is this love that I have let down all

                    guards

                          walls

                                shields

for so that I may someday
understand what it really means
to love a man
as I love my own child—
Unconditionally & without fear;
passion unlimited.

One lover had me in the dark & kept me there.
Another lover beckoned me to the light.
It is in the light that I wish to remain
& discover all that love, in its vast horizons
has to offer my soul.

LOVE

I have come
to the realization
that no man
on earth will
ever be able
to comprehend the
depths of love
I have to
offer. For I
am a stranger
to myself when
it comes to
this. My love
flows like water,
reaching levels deep
beyond the surface.
My love
expands
contracts
opens again
in the presence
& shape of
the lover before me—
Meeting & exceeding
what he offers
proudly as his
all. My love, wild
& open, shy
& wanting, spills
over, tripping over
my tongue, racing

ahead of my
heart & causing
me to lose
touch with myself.
But it is
myself that I
most want to
be with
sit with
allow to breathe.

No labels, without words.

What does
I love you
really mean anyway?
These three words
can never truly
express what happens to my
mind
body
soul
when my eyes
& spirit connect
with another traveler
along the journey—
A traveler, who,
like me, is
in search for
something
deeper
ethereal
undefined.

The truth is,
I haven't a
clue what love
is. But I now
know I have
the courage to
not speak these
three words again
for they betray
me & my very essence.
They go against
what I know
to be true:
words cannot define
Love, words limit
what Love can
be. Love is
what I wish
to evolve into,
what I imagine
one day I
can become.

VIPASSANA POEMS

Love is easy,
Relationships are hard.
                —**Experience**

The thought of loving you,
& having you all to myself
makes my heart sing.
              —**Solo Performance**

Keep your head above the water
& hold onto your heart
as you wade the sea of love.
Fierce currents mark the journey
but soon your soul
will find rest
among the waves.
              —**Just Keep Swimming**

In my silence, joy & peace emerged.
Then pain; ever patient, ever flowing.
I moved freely among the waves &
cried.

—Crossing My Ocean of Misery

To find out what went wrong
between us, I had to take
responsibility.
In noble silence, I looked
inside myself & listened.

—Keeping it 100 while Dissolving the Ego

When we talk again, please
tell me how to love you.
With instructions,
my love can support
your growth as you be
the man you are always
BEcoming.

—Talk of Human Flourishing

Your lingering scent
makes me high.

—Love's Hangover

To heal, I will wrap
myself in quiet &
never speak your name
again.

—The Silent Treatment

He wasn't prepared for the love I had to offer.

I lied. To myself. To others.
The truth is I wasn't prepared
for the love I had to offer
until I spent some time alone
with the love I have for myself.

—My First Love

Be gentle with us.
We each just want to be loved.
—The Other

Here's my truth:

From the very beginning
you knew you couldn't
love me in the way
I deserve to be loved.

My love opens all
you seek to conceal.
For safety you run
& hide.

There is grace in not reaching
out to me. There is generosity
in your silence.
—Compassion in Distance

To meet me where I am,
you believe you have to
be a certain you.
	Just come.
We are always changing,
always becoming.
In time you will get there
& so will I.

—The Process

The long path to our love begins
with the first step in believing
it is worth the journey.

—The Walk
Inspired by the Afro Samurai

My heart is the terrace overlooking
my deep desire for you.
I have contemplated the jump,
but know that such a sweet act
will lead to so much misery.

—Practicing Detachment

Together, we are the product of
broken hearts & the brave
decision to return to love.
　　　　　—Life's Manufacturing Game

Fate is the thing that
returns to you after
you've mourned its loss.
　　　　　—Eternal Hope

You bring peace with you.
Joy comes when you arrive.
　　　　　—The Visit

I better understand why you
like torrential rain.
If we look closely
it allows us to see ourselves
more clearly.
　　　　　—Weathering the Storm

Loving you is like watching
the clouds dance to make way
for the sun after the rain.
                    —**The Simplest Joy**

The Breakup: *I miss all that is you*, I said.
The Reunion: *Likewise*, you replied.

You have a beautiful mind,
    I like how you think.
You have a great body,
    I like how you look.
But don't you know it is the
soul that you carry that I
have fallen in love with?
                    —**Soulmate**

We three have prepared you for every
love & loss in life.
                    —**Miscarriage Trinity**

There is clarity to be found in Silence
                    —The Listening Eye

I cannot help but to write.
It is how I think & know love.
It is how I exist.
                  —The Burden of the Pen

A daughter is a gift
from God that passes
through the womb of
the mother.

—For Olivia

Of all the marvelous people
in the world to meet, it is you
I am most interested
in knowing.

—Inner Me

You heeded my call &
found yourself, us.

—Silence

Talk less,
love more.

—The Heart

I was set free—
because I let go.
—YOLANDA SEALEY-RUIZ

Afterword

The historian Peter Brown famously characterized saints as people "for whom mourning was unthinkable." As we progress further into the twenty-first century, these words seem to be relevant now for another special category of people invested with an importance that both connects us to them and also separates us from them: our exes. In the case of saints, if we couldn't mourn them per se, then we did at least have other socially-approved ways of recognizing them after they were gone. In the case of our exes, things are less certain; if we are to follow the dictates of current tastes and mores, we may come to the conclusion that there is in fact no way of relating to them that receives society's imprimatur as "respectable." Perhaps this is one reason why the concept of "ghosting" rises like a specter before us: doing nothing is the only safe way to avoid what may be seen as improper relationality. Well, what indeed is a ghost if not what haunts us, and sometimes conveys to us important information from realms that are just beyond our own grasp? Into this lacuna of the spirits wades Yolanda Sealey-Ruiz's *Love from the Vortex & Other Poems*.

In the Summer of 2019 I was taking a class which incorporated three days with Professor Sealey-Ruiz. On the third day she mentioned that our discussions had caused her to reach out to an ex with whom she had not spoken in some time. It is small moments of honesty like this that allow us all to be real in the classroom. I made a mental note. Several months later, at a workshop, Sealey-Ruiz was discussing her own experiences and briefly mentioned two exes who had been important. Again, I made a mental note. It's not uncommon for academics to mention spouses, and the academics who become successful enough can even include digressions about husbands and wives in their published works, but for the unmarried and the divorced the people with whom they have shared their lives tend to remain, at least formally, unspeakable. Sealey-Ruiz is the first academic I ever remember talking about exes in public. At the time, I had no idea that she was working on a book of poetry unapologetically centered around exes. Even as I write this now, I can't think of a way to write it without it sounding strange, and that is the point: the strangeness of this topic, the rareness of it, the saying of what is otherwise unsayable, is precisely what makes it relevant.

Historically, of course, it is the difficult relationships that drove the engine of literature. The whole idea of courtly love in the Middle Ages is that one *can't* be with the person and probably shouldn't say that one wants to be with the person. Lost love, impossible love, love of someone or something one can't possibly understand, love of someone or something that can't possibly understand you, love that can not say that it is love, love that is in fact afraid of what it is: these are the kinds of dynamics that one may call the "problems of desire," and it is when it becomes a seemingly unresolvable problem that desire becomes most present and most real. Odysseus is most real when he is gazing over the edge of his own ship. Every mystic tradition is most real when it is most conversant with the impossibility of realizing its own focus.

When Sealey-Ruiz mentions things that are "not even safe to discuss/during a private conversation with/myself," she is acknowledging the difficulty of what she is undertaking. Refreshingly, she takes these limitations as a starting point and not an endpoint. It is very uncommon to find a book of poetry as frank as this one is. On a topic that others would simply avoid, or perhaps address only drenched in the safety of forced emotional distance, Sealey-Ruiz simply tells us how she feels. There is something really remarkable about this, and it must be seen to be believed.

What Sealey-Ruiz is doing here is genuinely liberating, not only for herself but for others. Back in the day one would have called the forced silence around relationships outside of state-sanctioned matrimony "heteronormative." Nowadays, the term seems less apt, but the idea persists that there are relatively narrow ways of relating and being that we are allowed to talk about, and then there are other ways of relating and being about which we can never be too open. It is, in a way, an act of radical honesty for Sealey-Ruiz to publish a book of poems about six exes, and to do so in a style that doesn't hide behind the usual forms of detachment. It is this kind of act that hopefully opens up a bit more space for all of us to say what is around us and to be what we are.

David Lennington, PhD

Epigraphs & Quotations

The quotes as attributed in this book belong to their respective copyright owners. Full citations and permissions contact details are provided below for further information.

Zelda Fitzgerald
Dorian Karchmar, DKar@WMEntertainment.com
Jay Mandel, JMan@WMEntertainment.com

Jennifer Elisabeth
Elisabeth, Jennifer. *BORN READY: Unleash Your Inner Dream Girl.* LULU.COM, 2011.

Martha Madeiros
Originally from the poem, "A Morte Devagar" by Martha Madeiros. Translation found in:
Cegarra Cervantes, Maria del Mar. *The Art of Loving a Three: Me, You, and Us.* 2015. Translation by Ines Múrias, HAKABOOKS, 2017.

Ursula K. Leguin
Le Guin, Ursula K. *The Lathe of Heaven.* Gateway, 2015.
Literary permissions: gc@cbltd.com

Esther Hicks
>   Jerry & Esther Hicks
>   www.AbrahamHicks.com
>   (830) 755-2299

Bob Marley
>   info@tuffgongworldwide.com

Alice Walker
>   Joy Harris Literary Agency
>   adam@joyharrisliterary.com

In Gratitude

This book would not have happened without the help & kindness of some wonderful people in my life. I thank them for bringing me joy, perspective, wisdom & peace. My most immediate gratitude goes to Team Vortex! My goodness, what an amazing group of people you are! Yael Rosenstock, you are an awesome human being & the best publisher any author can ask for! I thank God for us having met a few times—each time so wonderful—& finally putting us together to bring one of my biggest dreams into reality.

Caroline Rinaldy, your belief in this project, your indefatigable energy, awesome talent, & great personality were consistent from the start! Thank you for your brilliant mind & sharp eye!

19, what can I say? You are one of the most talented creative artists I have met! I am so grateful for how you shared your talent in generous ways, & created pieces of art that I love. I feel completely blessed by having you interpret the words that flowed from my heart in such powerful images.

Chrissy Ramkarran, it is your own beautiful words in your book of poetry, *Relic*, that made me realize just how amazingly lucky I am to have your editing skills grace my work. I loved my poetry even more after you spent time with it. Thank you for your talent, & for helping me fall more deeply in love with a genre that has afforded me a way to express my deepest desires, fears, & passions. I've learned so much from you!

I am grateful to J.M.D., E.R.C, A.R.R., V.S.S.E, L.D.M., & S.E.E. the six who met me along my journey to self love. In loving each of you, I have learned so much about the beauty that exists in the world. I am grateful for your inspiration. Without you, this book would not exist.

I have deep gratitude for Ahkilah Johnson & Lum Fube who helped me get so many of these poems out of my journal, off of text messages, & from digital voice memos into one document. I hope you feel that the "grunt" work was worth it. These poems would not be in book form without the two of you.

Willy Mosquera, there would be no audiobook if not for you & Yael. Thank you for your patience, guidance, & brilliance! 11:11!

David Lennington, thank you for writing an Afterword that has offered me a new lens, & given me a new appreciation for my experience with the six.

Thank you Elsie (Mom), & Eddie (my late dad) for raising me. Mom, I don't know how you did it, but you took care of the three of us & provided the space where we could flourish into the people we are today. Thank you for taking me to all of those storytelling contests, listening to my first books & poems when I was a child. You believed in me & taught me to believe in myself.

Thank you, Olivia, for loving me & being the best daughter any mother could ask for. I learn so much from you about love & patience. Thank you for your grace.

Thank you, Donna & David, for loving me & always believing that your little sister would grow up & write something. I love you.

Miranda, you are the poet (along with Gwendolyn Brooks, Langston Hughes, Rupi Kaur, Nayyirah Waheed) who inspires me most. I love you.

Suzanne C. Carothers, thank you for being an incredible guide & a beautiful friend in my life for all these years.

Gholdy E. Muhammad, you are the best friend a girl could have. I am grateful for our trips, laughter, & CFB moments! But most importantly, as it relates to this project, I thank you for listening to just about every poem in this book. You listened patiently, critically—sometimes before dawn in the morning, & often late at night. You sat with me through the laughter & tears that produced these poems, pushed me in my faith in God, & convinced me to just go to sleep. You are right: it is "always better in the morning."

Richard Haynes, Shamari Reid, Angel Acosta, Brennan DuBose, Anna Urrea, Cluny & Selina Lavache, Lalitha Vasudevan, Laura Smith, Felicia Mensah, & Erica Walker, you showed up in my life just a short time ago, & you've made an impact that will last forever.

Carmen Kynard & Avon Connell, you have been my best friends & sisters for so long. Thank you for loving me in the way you have & the way you do.

Darrell Hucks, thank you for being my brother & my dear friend.

Perry Greene & H. Rich Milner, IV, thank you for being beautiful mentors & friends to me for so many years.

Nayyirah Waheed & Rupi Kaur—thank you for the everlasting inspiration.

To further family & friends who have pushed, supported, & loved me at various points in my life, I extend immense gratitude: Willie S.D. Walton, The Walton Family (Exree (deceased), Senora, Winifred, Tanya, Helena, & Sandy), The Ruiz Family (Andrew, Crystal, Chepe, CJ, Chris, Irene (deceased), Lisa & Rahmel), Lorenzo Martinez, Maddie Giambrone,

Justin Pertuz, The Chomas (Anna (deceased), Luba, Mary, Theresa, Natalie (deceased), & Bobby), The Chamblisses (Betty, Elsie, Alman, Norman, Chase, Grace, Ashiya), Lionel Horry, Bruce Diggs, Betty, Cathy, & Andrew Montalvo, The Pattersons (George, Michelle, Irma, & Oliver (deceased)), Juanita Johnson-Bailey, Elza Dinwidde Boyd, Herb Boyd, Don Rojas, Alasia Harris, Betty Arrington, Simeon Etta, Maria Colon, Taylor Turntime, Derek Koen, Ouida Washington, Umar Edwards, Salah Salaam, Christina Seda Acosta, Christopher Emdin, Esther Ohito, Iesha Jackson, Wanda Watson, Keisha Mcintosh Allen, Maryam Alikhani, Kanene Holder, Mariel Buque, Justin Coles, Adam Falkner, Gladston "Patrick" Williamson, Vincent Deas, Damaris Dunn, The Loves (Bettina, Chelsea, Chanson & Lauren), Lonice Eversly, Ivory Toldson, Chance Lewis, Sonya Horsford, Terrie Watson, Rosa Rivera McCutchen, David Johns, Lyle Yorks, Jacqueline Woodson, Tonya Leslie, Valerie Kinloch, Limarys Caraballo, Jamila Lyiscott, Danny Martinez, Sandra Quinones, Ramon Martinez, Latrise Johnson, Sybil Durand, Margarita Gomez, Maneka Brooks, Juan Guerra, Marc Lamont Hill, Michele Meyers, Kimberly Parker, Tim San Pedro, Melody Zoch, Detra Price-Dennis, Marcelle Haddix, Pedro Noguera, Travis Bristol, Marcelle Mentor, Matt Gonzales, Tracey Flores, Anderson Smith, Aubrey Lynch, Jennifer Cahill McLaughlin, Min Cho, The Boomers (Cecila, Donna, Iris, Lisa & Tash), William Greene, Charles Macklin, Rene Pena, Monique Weston, Edwin Blount, Janice Robinson, Olga Hubbard, Eustace Johnson, Sylvia Simpson, Mona Dixon, Ed Adjapong, s.j. Miller, Cleveland

Hayes, Ed Brockenbrough, Kisha Woods, Ernest Morrell, Ebony Elizabeth Thomas, Ebony McGee, The Crespos (Sam, Shawnte & Nyla), L.D. Martinez, Jonathan Deutsch, Erik Cork, Chezare Warren, Travis Bristol, Reshma Ramkellawan-Arteaga, Raven Wilhem, Yamilka Roque, Marsha Thorne, Norman Hoyte, Shelly Chin, Ty Defoe, Daniel Banks, Jamie Parker, Jennifer Banks, Terez Rollins, Dena Simmons, Micia Mosely, Kim White Smith, Liz Murray, James Scanlon, Maggie Scanlon, Joe Rogers, Mellie Torres, Moises Lopez, Jason Feldman, The Goodens (Mark, Angela & Nia), Vincent Jones II, Rahmell Peebles, Dierdre Hollman, Moira Pirsch, Lelani Rivera, JinJuan Gao, Jim McGreevy, Noah Gordon, Noah Golden, Erik Nolan, Tal Siegal, Jeremy Martin, Lee Bell, Cameron Rasmussen, Tiffany Nyachae, Vusa Sibandi, Abiola Farinde, Tia Madkins, Amber Pabon, Adisa Ajamu, Reverend Alfonso Wyatt, Allison Skerrett, Alquena Reed, Andre Harper, Brian Mooney, Bryan Ripley Crandall, Joseph Rodriquez, Gerald Campano, Carmen Martinez Roldan, Maria Paula Ghiso, Cameron McCarthy, Carol Telpha, Charan P. Morris, Cheryl Matias, Judy Yu, Elaine Perlman, James Garner, Joseph Levine, Khalil G. Muhammad, Phillip Smith, Cynthia Dillard, Duane Bruce, Kecia McManus, Maria Muhammad, Akillah Muhammad, Lauren Kelly, Nicole Mirra, Antero Garcia, Madeline Villanueva, Danielle & Naomi Filipiak, Sam Roberts, Saidiya Hartman, Ileana Jiminez, Jennifer Boykins, Adam Alvarez, Paul Forbes, Ingrid Chung, Anderson Smith, Shannon Waite, Rema Ella, Bradley Cutler, Ronald Schwalb, Terry Flennaugh, & those whose names may not be mentioned here — please know that I love you & I am grateful for who you have been to me.

I am also grateful to great people within these institutions who have also shown me love & support: Vipassana Meditation Center, Teachers College, Columbia University (Arts & Humanities Department, English Education Program, Office of Teacher Education, & Peace Corps Program), NCTE CNV, The Schomburg Junior Scholars Program, Sisters of the Academy (SOTA), Upfit Academy, New York City Department of Education, & New York City Men Teach Program.

Khalilah Brann—I really miss you.

Finally, thank you, reader. I am so happy this book is in your hands, may the poems touch your heart.

About the Book

Love from the Vortex & Other Poems is poet and scholar-activist Yolanda Sealey-Ruiz's first full-length collection. An archeological exploration of love and intimacy, the book charts her journey of finding and losing love over the span of three decades with six men who came into her life at various times. Sealey-Ruiz offers a universal take on what can happen when one seeks love and connection with others, and the lessons that follow when the connection and love are lost. Revealing moments of happiness, fantasy, frustration, and eventually the dissolution of relationships, the book moves beyond these anticipated stages to moments of grace and beauty that come with the discovery and practice of self-love, and a fuller understanding of what it means to truly love someone as you love yourself.

For more on the concept of the
Archeology of the Self by Yolanda Sealey-Ruiz, visit
https://www.yolandasealeyruiz.com/

About the Author

Yolanda Sealey-Ruiz is a poet & award-winning professor of English Education at Teachers College, Columbia University. A literacy educator for over two decades, she travels around the country speaking with fellow educators about race, culturally responsive pedagogy, & the power of love in education. She is the daughter of Elsie Sealey & (the late) Edgar Sealey, the sister of David & Donna, the mother of Olivia, & the best friend of Gholdy. Yolanda is a woman who loves God & still believes in love.